Long-Legged Friends

Long-Legged Friends

Crochet Creatures to Create and Cuddle

Hisako and Shizue Okawa

**Andrews McMeel
Publishing, LLC**

Kansas City • Sydney • London

SHIRO TO KURO NO AMIGURUMI by Hisako and Shizue Okawa
Copyright © Hisako and Shizue Okawa 2009

Original Japanese edition published by EDUCATIONAL FOUNDATION BUNKA GAKUEN BUNKA PUBLISHING BUREAU.

Publisher of the original Japanese edition: Sunao Oonuma
Art direction and design: Yukiko Inoue
Photography: Miwa Kumon
Layout: Satoshi Tanaka, Yoko Ogasawara
Technical editor: Chihiro Nishida
Illustrations: Shizue Okawa
Typography design of the Japanese edition: Mizuki Okawa
Editor of the original Japanese edition: Norie Hirai (BUNKA PUBLISHING BUREAU)

English edition published by arrangement with EDUCATIONAL FOUNDATION BUNKA GAKUEN BUNKA PUBLISHING BUREAU
through The English Agency (Japan) Ltd.

English Language rights, translation, and production by World Book Media, LLC
Email: info@worldbookmedia.com

Translated by Kyoko Matthews
English language editor: Lindsay Fair

Andrews McMeel Publishing, LLC
an Andrews McMeel Universal company
1130 Walnut Street, Kansas City, Missouri 64106

www.andrewsmcmeel.com

12 13 14 15 16 WRL 10 9 8 7 6 5 4 3 2 1

ISBN: 978-1-4494-1751-2

Library of Congress Control Number: 2011944592

Caution: Many of the dolls have small, removable parts. Please exercise caution when creating the dolls for use by children, and always supervise children while they play with dolls made with removable parts.

ATTENTION: SCHOOLS AND BUSINESSES
Andrews McMeel books are available at quantity discounts with bulk purchase for educational, business, or sales promotional use. For information, please e-mail the Andrews McMeel Publishing Special Sales Department:
specialsales@amuniversal.com

Introduction

"What kind of animal is this!?" complains my 85-year-old mother while she crochets. She has been crocheting for many decades, and I have to keep a watchful eye on her as I draw my own designs and steer her. With her fast pace, a dog would quickly become a pig if I turned my back or started daydreaming.

"I thought this design looked more like a pig because it's chubby," says my mother. It is difficult to change this stubborn lady who does not want to start over once she's started. Her work ethic is a perfect match for my creative vision. We hope you enjoy this book—and these projects—as much as we enjoyed writing it!

Contents

Fuzzy Rabbit White rabbit with black polka dots

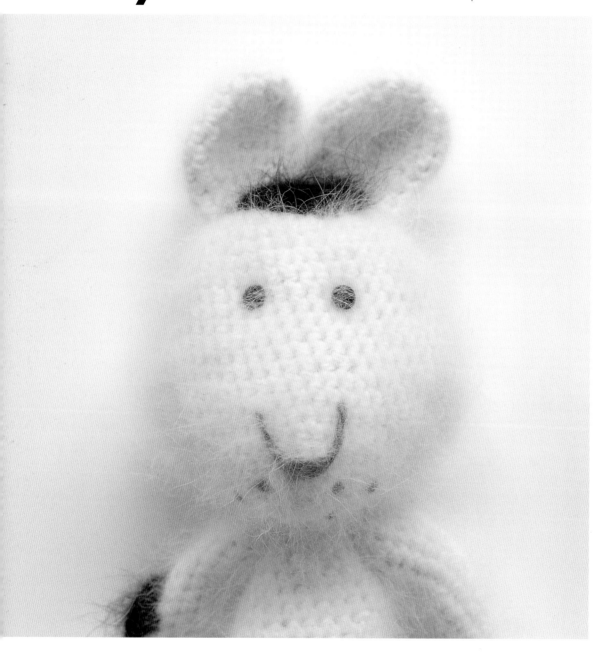

Instructions → page 52

Fuzzy Rabbit Black rabbit with white polka dots

Instructions → page 52

Fuzzy Rabbit Too

Black rabbit with white stripes

Instructions → page 52

Curly-Tailed
Cat Shown in black

Curly-Tailed Cat Shown in white

Instructions → page 56

Furry Bear White bear with black stripes

Furry Bear Black bear with gray polka dots

Instructions → page 60

Striped Bird

In mixed yarn

Striped Bird

In mohair yarn

Instructions → page 64

Little Ones

Instructions → page 68

Spotted Bull

Instructions → page 78

Fluffy Poodle

Instructions → page 82

Zigzag Pig

Instructions → page 84

Traveling Clothes

Materials, Tools, and Techniques

The materials and tools list is very simple: all you need is a crochet hook and some yarn to get started. A few other items will help you finish the job quickly and easily.

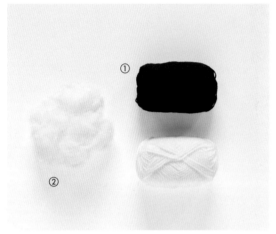

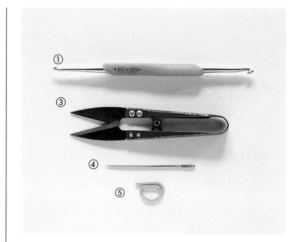

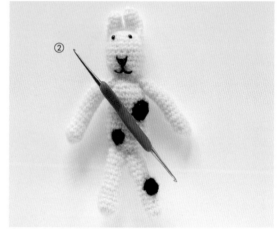

Materials

1. **Yarn:** Most of the animals call for black and white fingering-weight (#1 superfine) wool yarn. For added texture, many also use specialty yarns, such as angora, mohair, chenille, bouclé, and loop yarn. Feel free to experiment with different yarns to achieve your desired look and feel.

2. **Stuffing:** Use cotton or polyester stuffing to add shape to your critters.

3. **Eye buttons:** Sew on eye buttons for the eyes. There are a variety of different sizes available. From left to right: ½" (13 mm), ⅜" (10 mm), ⅓" (8 mm), ¼" (6 mm), and ⅛" (3 mm).

Tools

1. **C/2 (2.75 mm) crochet hook:** All of the animals, except the little ones, are made with a size C/2 (2.75 mm) crochet hook.

2. **B/1 (2.25 mm) crochet hook:** For the littlest animals, use a size B/1 (2.25 mm) crochet hook. Depending on the way you crochet, you can use a size C/2 (2.75 mm) hook if your gauge feels too tight.

3. **Scissors:** Use small thread clippers to cut the yarn.

4. **Yarn needle:** Use a yarn needle to sew the parts together, to attach eyes, and to embroider.

5. **Stitch ring marker:** It is difficult to count rows when you crochet in a spiral, so a ring marker helps you keep track.

Crochet Patterns and Charts

In this book, the crochet instructions for each animal are provided in two different ways: patterns and charts. The pattern contains symbols, while the chart uses numbers. Both versions contain the same information, but you may find that one is easier to follow than the other based on personal preference. The diagram below explains how to read both versions of instructions:

Pattern

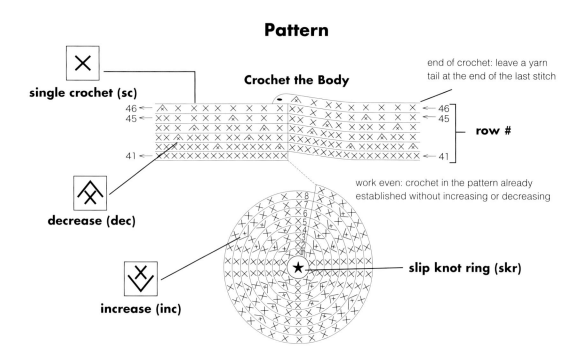

single crochet (sc)

decrease (dec)

increase (inc)

Crochet the Body

end of crochet: leave a yarn tail at the end of the last stitch

row #

work even: crochet in the pattern already established without increasing or decreasing

slip knot ring (skr)

Chart

Body		
row	sc	
46	18	(−2)
45	20	(−2)
44	22	(−4)
43	26	(−4)
42	30	(−4)
41		
⟩	34	work even
8		
7	34	(+4)
6	30	(+4)
5	26	(+4)
4	22	(+4)
3	18	(+4)
2	14	(+4)
1	10	skr

row #

single crochet

Negative numbers indicate decrease.

Positive numbers indicate increase.

slip knot ring
(Refer to basic crochet stitches on page 46.)

Basic Crochet Stitches

Slip Knot

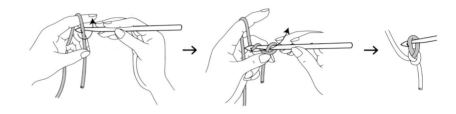

Slip Knot Ring (skr)

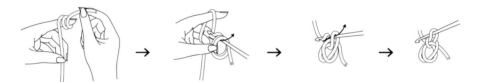

Wrap the yarn twice over the finger.

Slide the ring out and bring the yarn end to the front.

Insert the hook in the ring and draw up the loop.

Yarn over and draw up the loop again, and tighten.

Slip knot is not counted as a stitch.

Chain Stitch (ch)

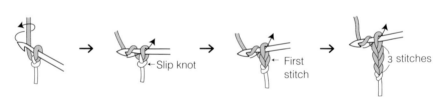

←Slip knot

← First stitch

3 stitches

The slip knot is not counted as a stitch except when working with thick yarn or unless with special instructions.

Slip Stitch (Sl st)

Single Crochet (sc)

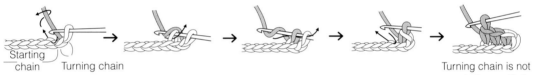

Starting chain   Turning chain

Use one chain stitch as turning chain.

Turning chain is not counted as a stitch.

Increase (inc)
Two single crochets in one stitch.

2 stitches

1 stitch

Increase one stitch is complete.

Decrease (dec)
Single crochet two stitches together.

1 stitch

Decrease one stitch is complete.

How to Make a Long-Legged Friend

Crochet

These stuffed friends are made using only two crochet stitches: chain and single crochet. In this method, you simply crochet in a continuous line, like a spiral staircase, always crocheting into the previous "spiral" to shape the animals without using turning chains. Each body part is crocheted separately then sewn together. When crocheting, leave a yarn tail at the end of the last stitch—this will make it easy to sew the parts together.

You can crochet the arms, legs, and bodies of these critters to whatever length you prefer—it's not necessary to follow the pattern exactly. Enjoy playing with different yarns, colors, and designs when creating your own animals.

Stuff

Use cotton or polyester stuffing to fill each body part according to the instructions for the specific animal you are making. One cozy technical note: the less stuffing you use, the softer the dolls will be.

Embellish

Attach the eyes and embroider the face to give your animal some personality. A few simple embroidery stitches are used, including the French knot, satin stitch, and fly stitch. Refer to page 50 for descriptions of these stitches.

Assemble

Thread the needle with a yarn tail and sew the body parts together using a whipstitch (refer to page 50). Once a seam is complete, fasten off the yarn, weave in the end, and trim the excess.

Anatomy of a Long-Legged Friend

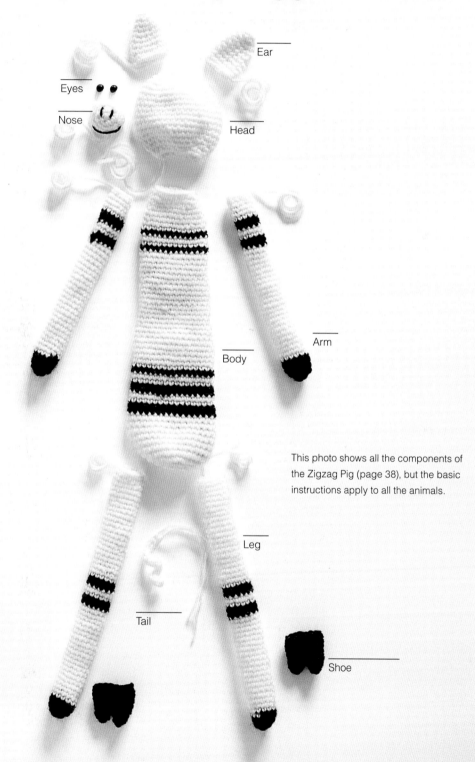

Eyes

Nose

Ear

Head

Body

Arm

This photo shows all the components of the Zigzag Pig (page 38), but the basic instructions apply to all the animals.

Leg

Tail

Shoe

Finishing Touches

In order to give your long-legged friend some personality, you'll want to add a few finishing touches, including eyes, embroidered facial features, and accessories. The instructions will note the finishing touches needed for each animal, but feel free to play with these details to design your perfect friend.

Attach the Eyes

Most of the animals have buttons as eyes. For light colored animals, the eye buttons are sewn to the head directly. For the dark colored animals use the following technique, which involves light felt circles, to make the eyes stand out:

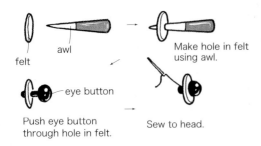

felt · awl · Make hole in felt using awl.

eye button · Push eye button through hole in felt. · Sew to head.

Embroider the Facial Features

Embroidery is the perfect way to create facial features for the animals. The following hand stitches are used to embroider and assemble the long-legged friends.

Fly stitch: Also known as the Y-stitch, this stitch is composed of a V-shaped loop anchored by a vertical straight stitch. This stitch forms the mouth of many of the creatures.

French knot: An embroidery stitch created by wrapping the yarn around the needle three times, then inserting the needle back into the fabric at the point where the needle emerged. This stitch is great for making whiskers.

Hemstitch: A nearly invisible stitch useful for joining fabric edges together. This stitch is used when making accessories, such as shoes.

Satin stitch: An embroidery technique composed of parallel rows of straight stitches positioned close together. This stitch is often used for noses.

Straight stitch: Also known as the running stitch, this is the most basic stitch, made by passing the needle in and out of the fabric.

Whipstitch: An overcast stitch used to join two pieces of fabric together. This stitch is also used to assemble the long-legged friends.

Add Accessories

Give your long-legged friend some style with the accessory designs featured in this book, which include shoes, scarves, hats, and bags. For a whimsical touch, embellish the accessories with pom-poms.

Make Pom-Poms:

1. Cut out two cardboard circle templates, slightly larger than the desired diameter of the finished pom-pom.

2. Cut a small hole in the center of each circle. Stack the templates on top of each other.

3. Tightly wind yarn around the templates, traveling through the center hole and the outer edge, until completely covered.

4. Insert scissors between the two templates and cut the yarn wound around the outer edge.

5. Tie a piece of yarn around the pom-pom center and knot to secure. Cut the cardboard templates away and remove.

6. Trim the pom-pom as desired to make it round and fluffy.

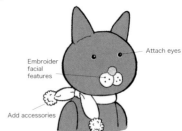

Attach eyes

Embroider facial features

Add accessories

For this book, Shizue Okawa, an illustrator, drew her designs for the animals and her 85-year-old mother Hisako crocheted them just by following the drawings. Hisako crochets lightning fast, but occasionally she stops to check the size of an animal by comparing it to her daughter's design. The length of the arms and legs, or the body shape of the finished animals is always different, but that just makes them all the more unique. It's not necessary to follow the pattern for each animal exactly. Enjoy making your own long-legged friends with whatever stripes, spots, and colors you'd like.

Fuzzy Rabbit

Project shown on page 8

Materials

Yarn

White Rabbit with Black Polka Dots:
    ivory angora for body, 444 yards (125 g) of worsted-weight (#4 medium)
    black angora for polka dots, small amount of worsted-weight (# 4 medium)
    gray angora for embroidery, small amount of worsted-weight (#4 medium)

Black Rabbit with White Polka Dots:
    black angora for body, 444 yards (125 g) of worsted-weight (#4 medium)
    white angora for polka dots, small amount of worsted-weight (#4 medium)
    gray angora for embroidery, small amount of worsted-weight (# 4 medium)

Black Rabbit with White Stripes:
    black angora for body, 444 yards (125 g) of worsted-weight (#4 medium)
    white angora for stripes, small amount of fingering-weight (# 4 medium)
    gray angora for embroidery, small amount of worsted-weight (# 4 medium)

Shoes for White Rabbit:
    black wool, 44 yards (10 g) of fingering-weight (#1 superfine)

Shoes for Black Rabbits:
    gray wool, 44 yards (10 g) of fingering-weight (#1 superfine)

Notions

Two ¼" (6 mm) black eye buttons

Two ⅜" (1 cm) white felt circles (for black rabbits only)

Polyester stuffing

Hook

C/2 (2.75 mm)

White Rabbit with Black Polka Dots

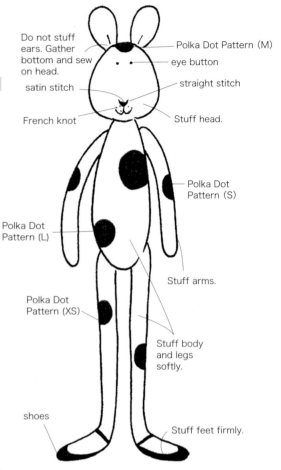

- Do not stuff ears. Gather bottom and sew on head.
- Polka Dot Pattern (M)
- eye button
- satin stitch
- straight stitch
- French knot
- Stuff head.
- Polka Dot Pattern (S)
- Polka Dot Pattern (L)
- Stuff arms.
- Polka Dot Pattern (XS)
- Stuff body and legs softly.
- shoes
- Stuff feet firmly.

Height: 22¾" (58 cm)

Make the Fuzzy Rabbit

1. Crochet each part. Make sure to crochet the feet before the legs as they will be joined together as you work.

2. Stuff each part, except the ears. Make sure to use the wrong side of the single crochet as the outside fabric.

3. Attach the eyes. Shape the face and embroider the nose and mouth, as shown in the diagram above.

4. Sew all parts together, as shown on page 49.

5. For the polka dot rabbit, crochet the polka dots and sew them to the body as shown, or create your own fun pattern. For the striped rabbit, embroider lines with white yarn.

6. Slip the shoes onto the feet.

Embroider the Mouth

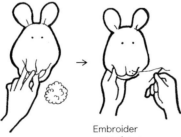

When stuffing, gather from inside.

Embroider nose above vertical line.

Black Rabbit with White Stripes

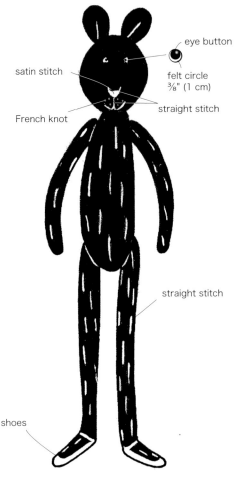

eye button

satin stitch

felt circle
3⁄8" (1 cm)

straight stitch

French knot

straight stitch

shoes

Height: 22¾" (58 cm)

Stuff in the same manner as the white rabbit.
For the Black Rabbit with White Polka Dots, use
this diagram for embroidering the face, but refer
to the white rabbit diagram for polka dot placement.

Crochet the Arms

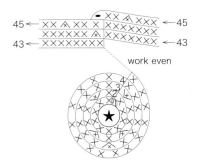

45 ←
43 ←
← 45
← 43

work even

Arms
Make 2

row	sc	
45	12	(−2)
44	14	(−1)
43		
⌇	15	work even
4		
3	15	(+1)
2	14	(+4)
1	10	skr

Crochet the Shoes

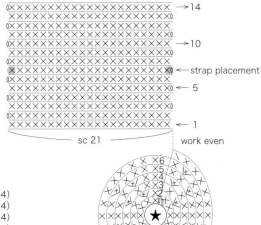

→ 14

→ 10

← strap placement

← 5

← 1

sc 21

work even

Shoes

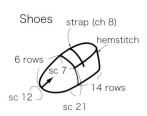

strap (ch 8)

hemstitch

6 rows

sc 7

sc 12

14 rows

sc 21

Shoes
Make 2

row	sc	
6	28	
5	28	(+4)
4	24	(+4)
3	20	(+4)
2	16	(+4)
1	12	skr

Crochet the Ears

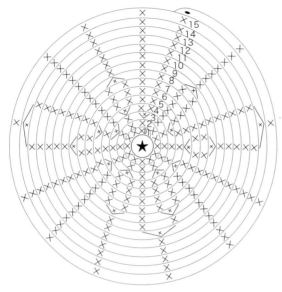

Ears
Make 2

row	sc	
15	13	
14	13	(−2)
13		
⑀		15 work even
11		
10	15	(−1)
9	16	
8	16	(−6)
7	22	
6	22	
5	22	(+2)
4	20	(+3)
3	17	(+5)
2	12	
1	12	skr

Crochet the Head

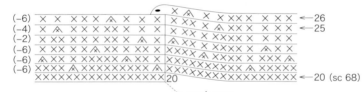

(−6) ←26
(−4) ←25
(−2)
(−6)
(−6)
(−6)
←20 (sc 68)

work even

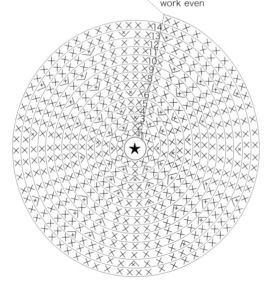

Head

row	sc	
26	38	(−6)
25	44	(−4)
24	48	(−2)
23	50	(−6)
22	56	(−6)
21	62	(−6)
20		
⑀		68 work even
14		
13	68	(+6)
12	62	(+6)
11	56	(+4)
10	52	(+4)
9	48	(+4)
8	44	(+4)
7	40	(+2)
6	38	(+4)
5	34	(+4)
4	30	(+6)
3	24	(+6)
2	18	(+6)
1	12	skr

Crochet the Body

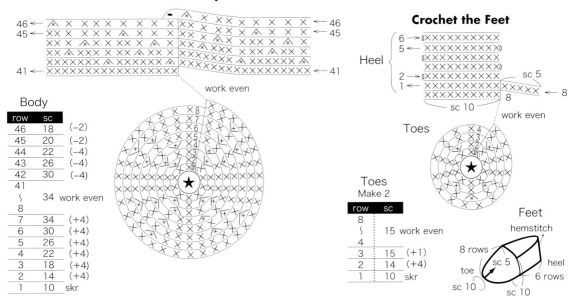

Body

row	sc	
46	18	(−2)
45	20	(−2)
44	22	(−4)
43	26	(−4)
42	30	(−4)
41		
⟨	34	work even
8		
7	34	(+4)
6	30	(+4)
5	26	(+4)
4	22	(+4)
3	18	(+4)
2	14	(+4)
1	10	skr

Crochet the Feet

Toes
Make 2

row	sc	
8		
⟨	15	work even
4		
3	15	(+1)
2	14	(+4)
1	10	skr

Crochet the Legs

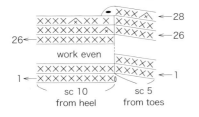

Legs
Make 2

row	sc	
28	12	(−2)
27	14	(−1)
26		
⟨	15	work even
1		

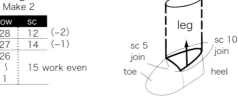

Crochet the Polka Dots

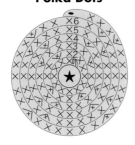

Polka Dot Pattern (XS)

row	sc	
1	12	work even

Polka Dot Pattern (S)

row	sc	
3	20	(+4)
2	16	(+4)
1	12	skr

Polka Dot Pattern (M)

row	sc	
5	28	(+4)
4	24	(+4)
3	20	(+4)
2	16	(+4)
1	12	skr

Dot Pattern (L)

row	sc	
6	32	(+4)
5	28	(+4)
4	24	(+4)
3	20	(+4)
2	16	(+4)
1	12	skr

Curly-Tailed Cat

Project shown on page 12

Materials

Yarn

White Cat:
   white chenille for body, 765 yards (125 g) of DK-weight (#3 light)
   black wool for embroidery, small amount of fingering-weight (#1 superfine)

Black Cat:
   black chenille for body, 765 yards (125 g) of DK-weight (#3 light)
   white chenille for mouth, small amount of DK-weight (#3 light)
   gray wool for nose, small amount of fingering-weight (#1 superfine)

Scarf for White Cat:
   black chenille, small amount of DK-weight (#3 light)

Scarf for Black Cat:
   ivory wool, small amount of fingering-weight (#1 superfine)

Notions

Two ½" (13 mm) black eye buttons (for white cat)
Two ⅜" (10 mm) black eye buttons (for black cat)
Two ⅜" (1 cm) white felt circles (for black cat)
Polyester stuffing

Hook

B/1 (2.25 mm)
C/2 (2.75 mm)

White Cat

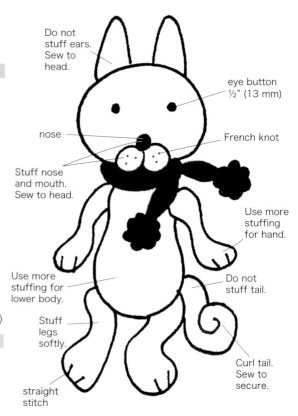

Do not stuff ears. Sew to head.

eye button ½" (13 mm)

nose

French knot

Stuff nose and mouth. Sew to head.

Use more stuffing for hand.

Use more stuffing for lower body.

Do not stuff tail.

Stuff legs softly.

Curl tail. Sew to secure.

straight stitch

Height: About 20" (51 cm)

Black Cat

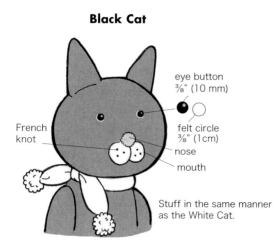

eye button ⅜" (10 mm)

French knot

felt circle ⅜" (1cm)

nose

mouth

Stuff in the same manner as the White Cat.

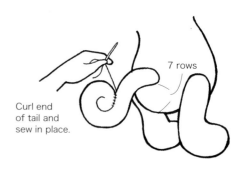

7 rows

Curl end of tail and sew in place.

Crochet the Ears

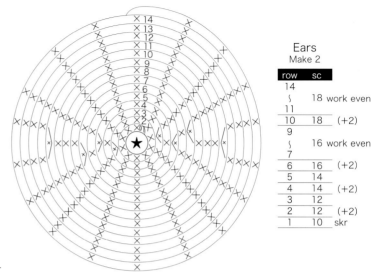

Make the Curly-Tailed Cat

1. Crochet each part. Use a C/2 (2.75 mm) crochet hook, except for the scarf for the Black Cat. Use a B/1 (2.25 mm) crochet hook for the scarf for the Black Cat.

2. Stuff each part, except the ears and the tail. Make sure to use the wrong side of the single crochet as the outside fabric.

3. Attach the eyes, nose, and mouth to the head. Embroider the mouth, as shown in the diagram on page 56.

4. Sew all parts together, as shown on page 49. Sew the tail to the back, according to the diagram on page 56.

5. Press the feet into a flat shape and embroider the toes, as shown in the diagram on page 56.

6. Tie the scarf around the cat's neck as a finishing touch.

Ears
Make 2

row	sc	
14		
⌇		18 work even
11		
10	18	(+2)
9		
⌇		16 work even
7		
6	16	(+2)
5	14	
4	14	(+2)
3	12	
2	12	(+2)
1	10	skr

Crochet the Head

(−3)		←28
(−3)		
(−5)		
(−5)		←25
(−5)		
(−5)		
	22	←22
		(sc 58)

work even

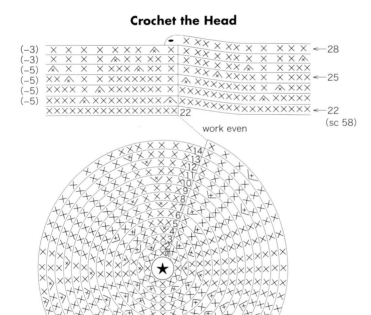

Head

row	sc	
28	32	(−3)
27	35	(−3)
26	38	(−5)
25	43	(−5)
24	48	(−5)
23	53	(−5)
22		
⌇		58 work even
15		
14	58	(+3)
13	55	(+3)
12	52	(+3)
11	49	(+3)
10	46	(+3)
9	43	(+3)
8	40	(+3)
7	37	(+3)
6	34	(+4)
5	30	(+4)
4	26	(+4)
3	22	(+4)
2	18	(+6)
1	12	skr

Crochet the Body

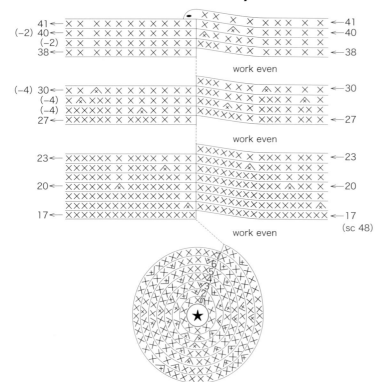

Body

row	sc	
41	26	
40	28	(−2)
39		(−2)
38	30	
⟨		work even
31	30	
30	34	(−4)
29	38	(−4)
28		(−4)
27	42	
⟨		work even
23	42	
22	44	(−2)
21	44	
20	46	(−2)
19	46	
18		(−2)
17		
⟨	48	work even
8		
7	48	(+4)
6	44	(+6)
5	38	(+6)
4	32	(+6)
3	26	(+6)
2	20	(+6)
1	10	skr

Crochet the Feet

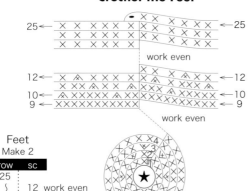

Feet
Make 2

row	sc	
25		
⟨	12	work even
13		
12	12	(−2)
11	14	(−4)
10	18	(−3)
9		
⟨	21	work even
4		
3	21	(+3)
2	18	(+6)
1	12	skr

Crochet the Hands

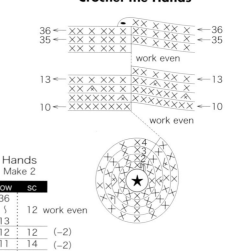

Hands
Make 2

row	sc	
36		
⟨	12	work even
13		
12	12	(−2)
11	14	(−2)
10		
⟨	16	work even
4		
3	16	(+2)
2	14	(+2)
1	12	skr

Crochet the Nose

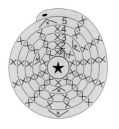

Nose

row	sc	
5	11	(−2)
4	13	
3	13	
2	13	(+3)
1	10	skr

Crochet the Mouth

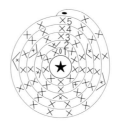

Mouth
Make 2

row	sc	
5	13	(−2)
4	15	
3	15	(+3)
2	12	(+3)
1	9	skr

Crochet the Scarf

Scarf for White Cat
Use C/2 (2.75 mm)
crochet hook.

Scarf for Black Cat
Use B/1 (2.25 mm)
crochet hook.

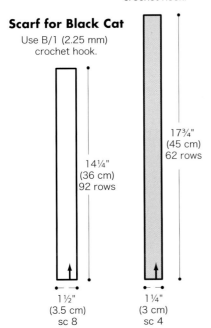

14¼"
(36 cm)
92 rows

17¾"
(45 cm)
62 rows

1½"
(3.5 cm)
sc 8

1¼"
(3 cm)
sc 4

Scarf

Crochet the Tail

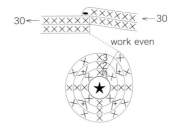

30← work even →30

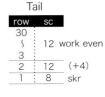

Tail

row	sc	
30		
∫	12	work even
3		
2	12	(+4)
1	8	skr

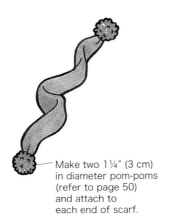

Make two 1¼" (3 cm)
in diameter pom-poms
(refer to page 50)
and attach to
each end of scarf.

Furry Bear

Project shown on page 16

Materials

Yarn

White Bear with Black Stripes:
white bouclé for body, 208 yards (80 g) of superbulky-weight (#6 superbulky)
black mohair for ears and stripes, 138 yards (35 g) of sport-weight (#2 fine)
black wool for embroidery, small amount of fingering-weight (#1 superfine)

Black Bear with Gray Polka Dots:
black angora for body, 409 yards (115 g) of sport-weight (#2 fine)
gray mohair for polka dots, small amount of sport-weight (#2 fine)
gray wool for embroidery, small amount of fingering-weight (#1 superfine)

Notions

Two ⅓" (8 mm) black eye buttons
Two ⅜" (1 cm) white felt circles (for black bear only)
Polyester stuffing

Hook

C/2 (2.75 mm)

White Bear with Black Stripes

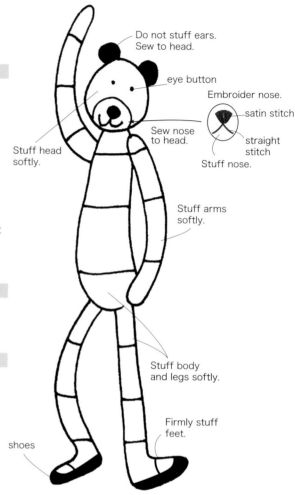

Do not stuff ears. Sew to head.
eye button
Embroider nose.
satin stitch
straight stitch
Sew nose to head.
Stuff nose.
Stuff head softly.
Stuff arms softly.
Stuff body and legs softly.
Firmly stuff feet.
shoes

Height: About 21¾" (55 cm)

Crochet the Head

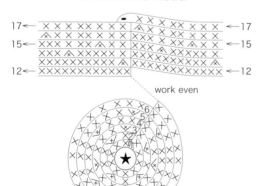

work even

Head

row	sc	
17	16	
16	16	(−2)
15	18	(−2)
14	20	(−2)
13	22	(−2)
12		
⌇	24	work even
6		
5	24	(+2)
4	22	(+4)
3	18	(+4)
2	14	(+4)
1	10	skr

Make the Furry Bear

1. Crochet each part. Make sure to crochet the feet before the legs as they will be joined together as you work. For the white bear, crochet the body, arms, and feet with stripes. For the black bear, crochet the polka dots and sew them to the body as shown, or create your own fun pattern.

2. Stuff each part, except the ears. Make sure to use the wrong side of the single crochet as the outside fabric.

3. Attach the eyes and nose to the head. Embroider the nose and mouth, as shown in the diagram.

4. Sew all parts together, as shown on page 49.

5. Slip the shoes onto the feet.

Black Bear with Gray Polka Dots

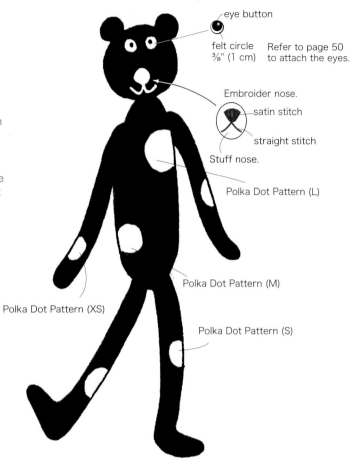

eye button

felt circle ³⁄₈" (1 cm)

Refer to page 50 to attach the eyes.

Embroider nose.
satin stitch
straight stitch

Stuff nose.

Polka Dot Pattern (L)

Polka Dot Pattern (M)

Polka Dot Pattern (S)

Polka Dot Pattern (XS)

Height: About 19¾" (50 cm)

Stuff in the same manner as the White Bear with Black Stripes.

Crochet the Ears

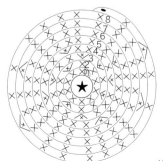

Ears
Make 2

row	sc	
8	18	(−2)
7	20	(−2)
6	22	
5	22	
4	22	(+4)
3	18	(+4)
2	14	(+4)
1	10	skr

＊Use black yarn for the White Bear with Black Stripes.

Crochet the Nose

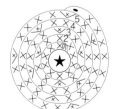

Nose

row	sc	
5	22	(+3)
4	19	(+3)
3	16	(+3)
2	13	(+3)
1	10	skr

Crochet the Feet

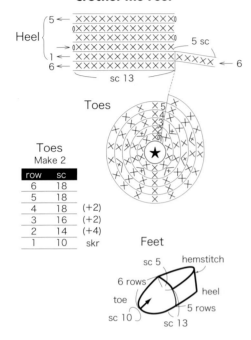

Heel

5 sc

5 ← ... ← 0
6 ← ... ← 6
sc 13

Toes
Make 2

row	sc	
6	18	
5	18	
4	18	(+2)
3	16	(+2)
2	14	(+4)
1	10	skr

Feet

sc 5 hemstitch
6 rows
toe heel
sc 10 5 rows
sc 13

Crochet the Legs

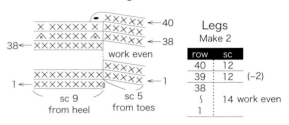

40 ←
38 ← 38
work even
1 ← 1
sc 9
from heel
sc 5
from toes

Legs
Make 2

row	sc	
40	12	
39	12	(−2)
38		
⌇	14 work even	
1		

Striped Leg Pattern for White Bear with Black Stripes

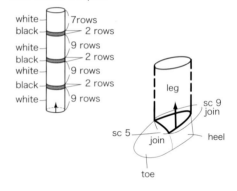

white — 7 rows
black — 2 rows
white — 9 rows
black — 2 rows
white — 9 rows
black — 2 rows
white — 9 rows

leg
sc 9 join
sc 5
join heel
toe

Crochet the Arms

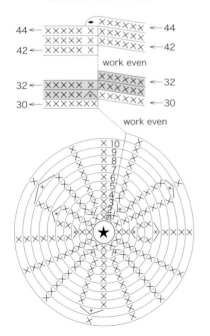

44 ← ← 44
42 ← ← 42
work even
32 ← ← 32
30 ← ← 30
work even

X 10
X 9
X 8
X 7
X 6
X 5
X 4
X 3
X 2
X 1

Arms
Make 2

row	sc	
44		
⌇	12 work even	
32		
31	12	(−1)
30		
⌇	13 work even	
10		
9	13	(−3)
8	16	
7	16	
6	16	(−2)
5	18	
4	18	
3	18	(+2)
2	16	(+4)
1	12	skr

Striped Arm Pattern for White Bear

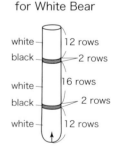

white — 12 rows
black — 2 rows
white — 16 rows
black — 2 rows
white — 12 rows

Crochet the Shoes

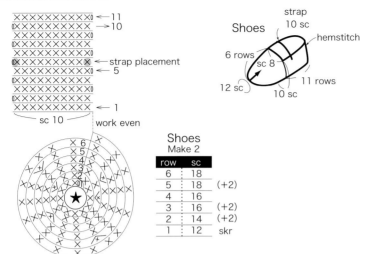

strap placement ← 5
← 11
→ 10
sc 10
work even
← 1

Shoes
strap 10 sc
hemstitch
6 rows
sc 8
11 rows
12 sc
10 sc

Shoes
Make 2

row	sc	
6	18	
5	18	(+2)
4	16	
3	16	(+2)
2	14	(+2)
1	12	skr

Crochet the Polka Dots for the Black Bear

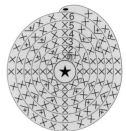

Polka Dot Pattern (XS)

row	sc	
1	12	skr

Polka Dot Pattern (S)

row	sc	
3	20	(+4)
2	16	(+4)
1	12	skr

Polka Dot Pattern (M)

row	sc	
5	28	(+4)
4	24	(+4)
3	20	(+4)
2	16	(+4)
1	12	skr

Polka Dot Pattern (L)

row	sc	
6	32	(+4)
5	28	(+4)
4	24	(+4)
3	20	(+4)
2	16	(+4)
1	12	skr

Crochet the Body

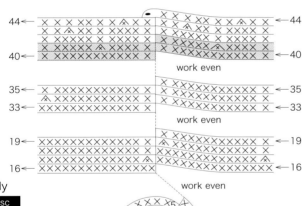

44 ← → 44
40 ← → 40
work even
35 ← → 35
33 ← → 33
work even
19 ← → 19
16 ← → 16
work even

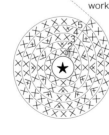

Body

row	sc	
44	20	(−2)
43	22	(−2)
42	24	
41	24	(−2)
40 ⌇ 35	26	
34	26	(−1)
33 ⌇ 19	27	work even
18	27	(−1)
17	28	(−2)
16 ⌇ 5	30	work even
4	30	(+6)
3	24	(+6)
2	18	(+6)
1	12	skr

Striped Body Pattern for White Bear with Black Stripes

white — 3 rows
black — 2 rows
white — 12 rows
black — 3 rows
white — 11 rows
black — 2 rows
white — 11 rows

Striped Bird

Project shown on page 20

Materials

Striped Bird in Mohair:
   ivory mohair for body, 196 yards (50 g) of sport-weight (#2 fine)
   black mohair for arms and stripes, 157 yards (40 g) of sport-weight (#2 fine)

Striped Bird in Mixed Yarn:
   white bouclé for body, 130 yards (50 g) of superbulky-weight (#6 superbulky)
   black mohair for arms and stripes, 157 yards (40 g) of sport-weight (#2 fine)

Scarf for Striped Bird in Mixed Yarn:
   black mohair, small amount of sport-weight (#2 fine)

Notions

Two ⅜" (10 mm) black eye buttons (for mohair bird)
Two ½" (12 mm) black eye buttons (for mixed yarn bird)
Polyester stuffing

Hook

C/2 (2.75 mm)

Striped Bird

Sew comb pieces to head (without stuffing).

eye button

Stuff head softly.

Do not stuff beak. Layer the two beak pieces and sew about ⅜" (1 cm) together.

Do not stuff arms.

Stuff body and legs softly.

Height: About 20"-21" (51-53 cm)

Crochet the Scarf

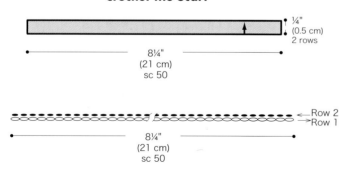

¼"
(0.5 cm)
2 rows

8¼"
(21 cm)
sc 50

←Row 2
←Row 1

8¼"
(21 cm)
sc 50

Make two 1¼" (3 cm) in diameter pom-poms (refer to page 50) and attach to each end of scarf.

Make the Striped Bird

1. Crochet each part.

2. Stuff each part, except the comb, beak, and arms. Make sure to use the wrong side of the single crochet as the outside fabric.

3. Attach the eyes, beak, and comb to the head.

4. Sew all parts together, as shown on page 49.

5. Tie the scarf around the bird's neck as a finishing touch.

Crochet the Beak

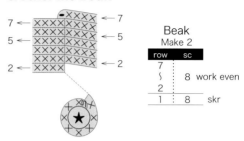

Beak
Make 2

row	sc	
7		
≀		8 work even
2		
1	8	skr

Crochet the Comb

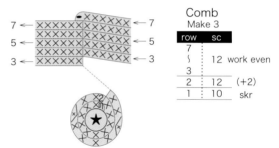

Comb
Make 3

row	sc	
7		
≀		12 work even
3		
2	12	(+2)
1	10	skr

Crochet the Head

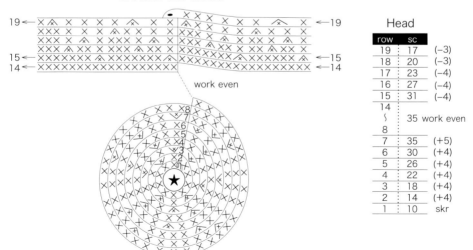

work even

Head

row	sc	
19	17	(−3)
18	20	(−3)
17	23	(−4)
16	27	(−4)
15	31	(−4)
14		
≀		35 work even
8		
7	35	(+5)
6	30	(+4)
5	26	(+4)
4	22	(+4)
3	18	(+4)
2	14	(+4)
1	10	skr

Crochet the Body

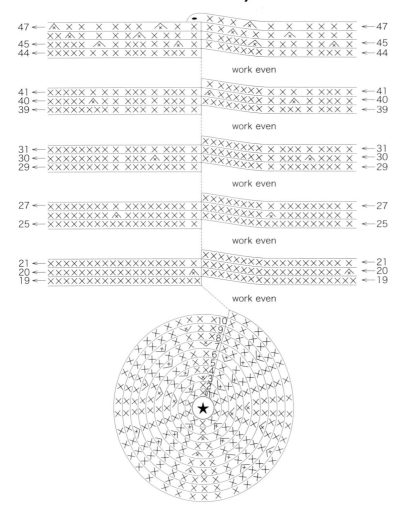

Body

row	sc	
47	20	(-3)
46	23	(−4)
45	27	(−4)
44		
∫		31 work even
41		
40	31	(−3)
39		
∫		34 work even
31		
30	34	(−2)
29		
∫		36 work even
27		
26	36	(−2)
25		
∫		38 work even
21		
20	38	(−2)
19		
∫		40 work even
10		
9	40	(+2)
8	38	(+4)
7	34	(+4)
6	30	(+4)
5	26	(+4)
4	22	(+4)
3	18	(+4)
2	14	(+4)
1	10	skr

Crochet the Arms

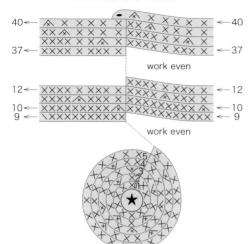

Arms
Make 2

row	sc	
40	12	(−2)
39	14	(−2)
38	16	(−2)
37 ≀ 12	18	work even
11	18	(−2)
10	20	(−2)
9 ≀ 5	22	work even
4	22	(+4)
3	18	(+4)
2	14	(+4)
1	10	skr

Arm

black

Hands

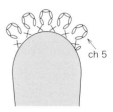

ch 5

To make the hands, ch 1, sc 1, ch 5 to make the loop, then sc back into the arm. Repeat the process to complete the hands.

Crochet the Legs

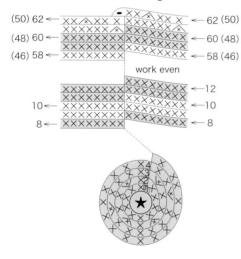

The numbers in ( ) are the number of rows for the Striped Bird in Mohair.

Do not cut the yarn when crocheting stripes.

Striped Leg Pattern for Bird in Mixed Yarn

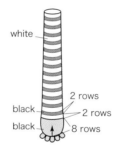

white

black
2 rows

black
2 rows

8 rows

Striped Leg Pattern for Bird in Mohair

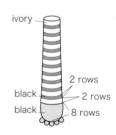

ivory

black
2 rows

black
2 rows

8 rows

Legs
Make 2

color	row	sc	
stripe pattern every 2 rows	62	12	(−2)
	61	14	(−2)
	60 ≀ 9	16	work even
	8 ≀ 4	16	work even
black	3	16	(+2)
	2	14	(+4)
	1	10	skr

Legs
Make 2

color	row	sc	
stripe pattern every 2 rows	50	12	(−2)
	49	14	(−2)
	48 ≀ 9	16	work even
	8 ≀ 4	16	work even
black	3	16	(+2)
	2	14	(+4)
	1	10	skr

Feet

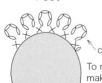

ch 5

To make the feet, ch 1, sc 1, ch 5 to make the loop, then sc back into the leg. Repeat the process to complete the feet.

Little Rabbit

Project shown on page 26

Materials

Yarn

Little White Rabbit:
    ivory mohair for body, 51 yards (13 g) of sport-weight (#2 fine)
    black mohair for polka dots and embroidery, small amount of sport-weight (#2 fine)

Little Black Rabbit:
    black mohair for body, 51 yards (13 g) of sport-weight (#2 fine)
    ivory mohair for polka dots, small amount of sport-weight (#2 fine)
    gray wool for embroidery, small amount of fingering-weight (#1 superfine)

Notions

Two ⅛" (3 mm) black eye buttons
Two ¼" (6 mm) white felt circles (for black rabbit)
Polyester stuffing

Hook

B/1 (2.25 mm)

Make the Little Rabbit

1. Crochet each part.
2. Stuff each part, except for the ears. Make sure to use the wrong side of the single crochet as the outside fabric.
3. Attach the eyes. Embroider the nose and mouth, as shown in the diagram below.
4. Sew all parts together, as shown on page 49.
5. Crochet the polka dots and sew them to the body as shown below, or create your own fun pattern.

Little White Rabbit

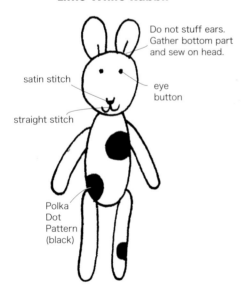

Do not stuff ears. Gather bottom part and sew on head.

satin stitch

eye button

straight stitch

Polka Dot Pattern (black)

Height: About 6¾" (17 cm)

Little Black Rabbit

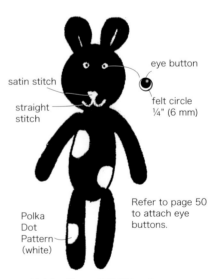

eye button

felt circle ¼" (6 mm)

satin stitch

straight stitch

Polka Dot Pattern (white)

Refer to page 50 to attach eye buttons.

Height: About 6¾" (17 cm)

Crochet the Legs

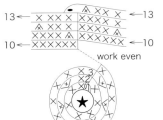

Legs
Make 2

row	sc	
13	8	(−1)
12	9	(−1)
11	10	(−2)
10		
⌇		12 work even
3		
2	12	(+5)
1	7	skr

Crochet the Ears

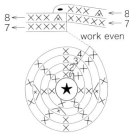

Ears
Make 2

row	sc	
8	8	(−2)
7		
⌇		10 work even
4		
3	10	(+2)
2	8	(+1)
1	7	skr

Crochet the Polka Dot

Polka Dot Pattern

row	sc	
1	13	skr

Crochet the Body

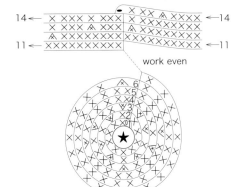

Body

row	sc	
14	16	(−1)
13	17	(−1)
12	18	(−2)
11		
⌇		20 work even
7		
6	20	(−2)
5	22	
4	22	(+2)
3	20	(+4)
2	16	(+6)
1	10	skr

Crochet the Arms

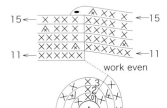

Arms
Make 2

row	sc	
15	8	(−1)
14	9	(−1)
13	10	
12	10	(−2)
11		
⌇		12 work even
3		
2	12	(+5)
1	7	skr

Crochet the Head

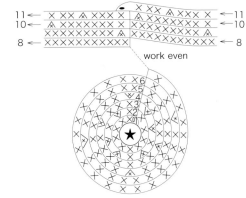

Head

row	sc	
11	16	(−2)
10	18	(−2)
9	20	(−2)
8		
⌇		22 work even
6		
5	22	(+2)
4	20	(+2)
3	18	(+2)
2	16	(+6)
1	10	skr

Little Cat

Project shown on page 26

Materials

Yarn

ivory mohair for body, 51 yards (13 g) of sport-weight (#2 fine)
black mohair for nose and scarf, small amount of sport-weight (#2 fine)
black wool for embroidery, small amount of fingering-weight (#1 superfine)

Notions

Two ⅛" (3 mm) black eye buttons
Polyester stuffing

Hook

B/1 (2.25 mm)

Make the Little Cat

1. Crochet each part.

2. Stuff each part, except the ears and nose. Make sure to use the wrong side of the single crochet as the outside fabric.

3. Attach the eyes, nose, and mouth to the head. Embroider the mouth, as shown in the diagram below.

4. Sew all parts together, as shown on page 49.

5. Tie the scarf around the cat's neck as a finishing touch.

Little Cat

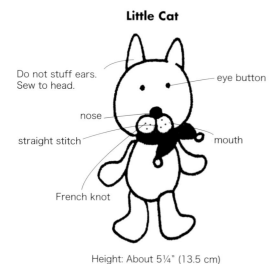

Do not stuff ears. Sew to head.

eye button

nose

straight stitch

mouth

French knot

Height: About 5¼" (13.5 cm)

Crochet the Scarf

← 1

sc 40

Leave yarn tails at each end of the scarf and tie in a knot to create fringe.

Crochet the Body

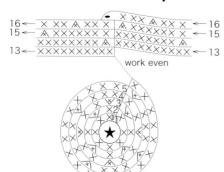

work even

Body

row	sc	
16	14	(−2)
15	16	(−2)
14	18	(−2)
13		
⌇	20 work even	
5		
4	20	(+4)
3	16	(+4)
2	12	(+4)
1	8	skr

Crochet the Tail

← 1

sc 10

Crochet the Arms

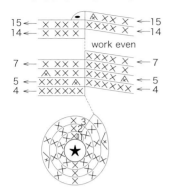

Arms
Make 2

row	sc	
15	8	(−1)
14		
≀	9	work even
7		
6	9	(−1)
5	10	(−2)
4	12	
3	12	(+2)
2	10	
1	10	skr

Crochet the Ears

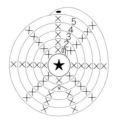

Ears
Make 2

row	sc	
5		
≀	9	work even
3		
2	9	(+1)
1	8	skr

Crochet the Nose

Nose

row	sc	
3	6	(−2)
2	8	
1	8	skr

Crochet the Legs

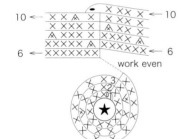

Legs
Make 2

row	sc	
10	8	(−1)
9	9	
8	9	(−2)
7	11	(−2)
6		
≀	13	work even
3		
2	13	(+2)
1	11	skr

Crochet the Mouth

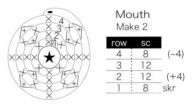

Mouth
Make 2

row	sc	
4	8	(−4)
3	12	
2	12	(+4)
1	8	skr

Crochet the Head

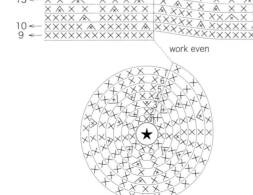

Head

row	sc	
13	13	(−4)
12	17	(−4)
11	21	(−3)
10	24	(−4)
9		
≀	28	work even
7		
6	28	(+2)
5	26	(+2)
4	24	(+5)
3	19	(+4)
2	15	(+4)
1	11	skr

Little Bear

Project shown on page 26

Materials

Yarn

Little White Bear:

ivory mohair for body, 51 yards (13 g) of sport-weight (#2 fine)

black mohair for stripes and embroidery, small amount of sport-weight (#2 fine)

Little Black Bear:

black mohair for body, 51 yards (13 g) of sport-weight (#2 fine)

ivory mohair for stripes, small amount of sport-weight (#2 fine)

gray wool for embroidery, small amount of fingering-weight (#1 superfine)

Notions

Two ⅛" (3 mm) black eye buttons
Two ¼" (6 mm) white felt circles (for black bear)
Polyester stuffing

Hook

B/1 (2.25 mm)

Make the Little Bear

1. Crochet each part.

2. Stuff each part, except the ears. Make sure to use the wrong side of the single crochet as the outside fabric.

3. Attach the eyes and nose to the head. Embroider the nose and mouth, as shown in the diagram below.

4. Sew all parts together, as shown on page 49.

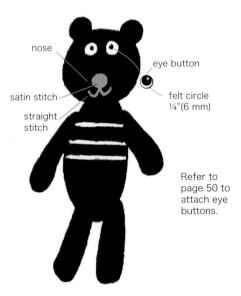

Little Black Bear

nose

eye button

satin stitch

felt circle ¼"(6 mm)

straight stitch

Refer to page 50 to attach eye buttons.

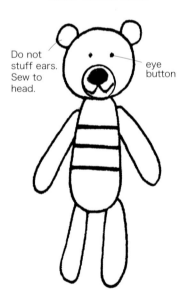

Little White Bear

Do not stuff ears. Sew to head.

eye button

Crochet the Head

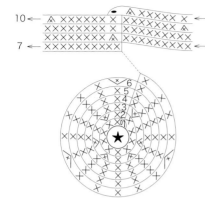

Head

row	sc	
10	15	(−2)
9	17	(−1)
8	18	(−1)
7	19	
6	19	(+3)
5		
∫		16 work even
3		
2	16	(+6)
1	10	skr

Crochet the Nose and Ears

Nose · Ears
Make 3 total

row	sc	
3	10	
2	10	
1	10	skr

Crochet the Legs

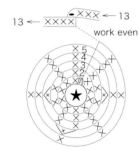

work even

Legs
Make 2

row	sc	
13		
∫		7 work even
5		
4	7	(−1)
3	8	(−2)
2	10	
1	10	skr

Crochet the Arms

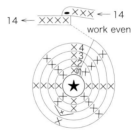

work even

Arms
Make 2

row	sc	
14		
∫		7 work even
4		
3	7	(−1)
2	8	
1	8	skr

Crochet the Body

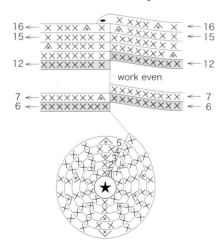

work even

Body

color	row	sc	
A	16	12	(−2)
	15	14	(−1)
	14	15	(−1)
	13	16	(−1)
B	12	17	
A	11	17	
	10	17	
B	9	17	
A	8	17	
	7	17	(−1)
B	6	18	
A	5	18	(−2)
	4	20	(+2)
	3	18	(+4)
	2	14	(+4)
	1	10	skr

White Bear
  Color A = Ivory   Color B = Black

Black Bear
  Color A = Black   Color B = Ivory

Striped Body Pattern

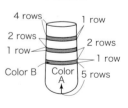

4 rows   1 row
2 rows   2 rows
1 row   1 row
Color B   Color A   5 rows

Little Bird

Project shown on page 26

Materials

Yarn

ivory mohair for body, 40 yards (10 g) of sport-weight (#2 fine)

black mohair for arms and stripes, 28 yards (7 g) of sport-weight (#2 fine)

black wool for beak, small amount of fingering-weight (#1 superfine)

Notions

Two ⅓" (8 mm) black eye buttons
Polyester stuffing

Hook

B/1 (2.25 mm)
C/2 (2.75 mm)

Make the Little Bird

1. Crochet each part. Use a B/1 (2.25 mm) crochet hook, except for the beak. Use a C/2 (2.75 mm) crochet hook for the beak.

2. Stuff each part, except the comb, beak, and arms. Make sure to use the wrong side of the single crochet as the outside fabric, except for the legs. Use the right side for the legs.

3. Attach the eyes, beak, and comb to the head.

4. Sew all parts together, as shown on page 49.

5. Sew the collar around the neck.

Little Bird

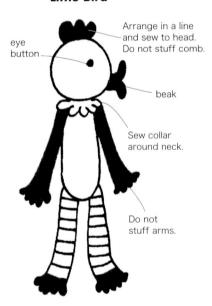

eye button

Arrange in a line and sew to head. Do not stuff comb.

beak

Sew collar around neck.

Do not stuff arms.

Height: About 6" (16.5 cm)

Crochet the Beak

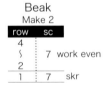

Beak
Make 2

row	sc	
4		
⌇	7	work even
2		
1	7	skr

Do not stuff beak. Layer the two beak pieces and sew about ⅜" (1 cm) together.

Crochet the Collar

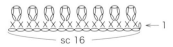

← 1

sc 16

Crochet the Head

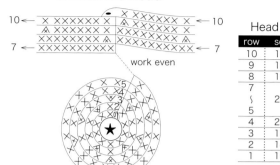

work even

Head		
row	sc	
10	16	
9	16	(−2)
8	18	(−2)
7		
⌇		20 work even
5		
4	20	(+2)
3	18	(+4)
2	14	(+4)
1	10	skr

Crochet the Comb

Comb Make 2		
row	sc	
3	7	(−1)
2	8	
1	8	skr

Crochet the Body

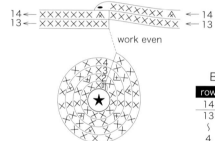

work even

Body		
row	sc	
14	16	(−2)
13		
⌇		18 work even
4		
3	18	(+3)
2	15	(+4)
1	11	skr

Crochet the Arms

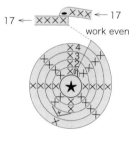

work even

Arms Make 2		
row	sc	
17		
⌇		7 work even
4		
3	7	(−1)
2	8	
1	8	skr

Crochet the Legs

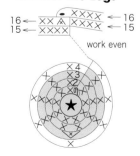

work even

Striped Leg Pattern

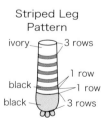

ivory — 3 rows
black — 1 row / 1 row
black — 3 rows

Legs Make 2			
color	row	sc	
	16	7	(−1)
black	15	8	
	14	8	
	13		
ivory	⌇		8 work even
	4		
	3	8	(−1)
black	2	9	
	1	9	skr

Hands and Feet

ch 1

To make the hands and feet, ch 1, sc 1, ch 5 to make the loop, then sc back into the arm or leg. Repeat the process to complete the hands and feet.

Little Bull

Project shown on page 26

Materials

Yarn

ivory mohair for body, 59 yards (15 g) of sport-weight (#2 fine)
black mohair for polka dots, small amount of sport-weight (#2 fine)

Notions

Polyester stuffing

Hook

B/1 (2.25 mm)

Make the Little Bull

1. Crochet each part.

2. Stuff each part, except the ears. Make sure to use the wrong side of the single crochet as the outside fabric.

3. To shape the cheeks, refer to page 78. Embroider the eyes, nose, mouth, and hands, as shown in the diagram below.

4. Sew all parts together, as shown on page 49.

5. Crochet the polka dot and sew it to the top of the head.

Little Bull

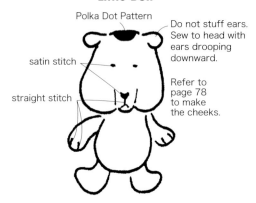

Polka Dot Pattern

Do not stuff ears. Sew to head with ears drooping downward.

satin stitch

Refer to page 78 to make the cheeks.

straight stitch

Height: About 5¼" (13.5 cm)

Crochet the Head

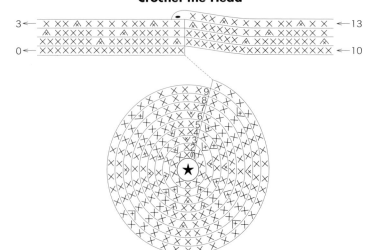

Head

row	sc	
13	26	(−4)
12	30	(−4)
11	34	(−4)
10	38	
9	38	
8	38	(+4)
7	34	(+2)
6	32	(+2)
5	30	(+2)
4	28	(+6)
3	22	(+6)
2	16	(+6)
1	10	skr

Crochet the Legs

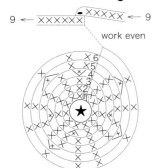

9 ← XXXXXX ⬛ XXXXX ← 9
work even

Legs
Make 2

row	sc	
9		
∫	11	work even
6		
5	11	(−4)
4	15	(+1)
3	14	(+2)
2	12	(+1)
1	11	skr

Crochet the Tail

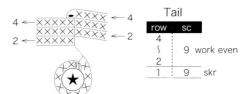

4 ← XXXXX ⬛ XXXX ← 4
XXXXXX XXXX
2 ← XXXXX ← 2

Tail

row	sc	
4		
∫	9	work even
2		
1	9	skr

Crochet the Arms

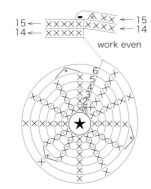

15 ← XXXXX ⬛ XXX ← 15
14 ← XXXXX XXX ← 14
work even

Arms
Make 2

row	sc	
15	8	(−1)
14		
∫	9	work even
7		
6	9	(−2)
5	11	(−1)
4		
∫	12	work even
2		
1	12	skr

Crochet the Ears

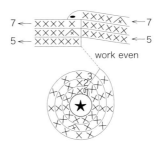

7 ← XXXX ⬛ XXXX ↖ ← 7
XXXXX XXXXX
5 ← XXXXXX ← 5
work even

Ears
Make 2

row	sc	
7	10	(−1)
6	11	(−1)
5		
∫	12	work even
3		
2	12	(+1)
1	11	skr

Crochet the Body

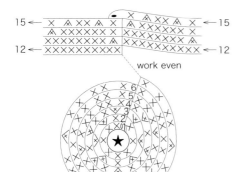

15 ← X ⋀ XX⋀ X ⬛ X ⋀⋀⋀X X → 15
⋀ XXXXX⋀ XXXXX XX ⋀
XXXXXX XXXXXXXX
12 ← XXXXXXX XXXXXXXXXX → 12
work even

Body

row	sc	
15	12	(−4)
14	16	(−2)
13	18	(−2)
12		
∫	20	work even
7		
6	20	(−2)
5	22	
4	22	(+2)
3	20	(+6)
2	14	(+6)
1	8	skr

Crochet the Polka Dot

Polka Dot Pattern

row	sc	
3	18	(+4)
2	14	(+4)
1	10	skr

Spotted Bull

Project shown on page 28

Materials

Yarn

white chenille for body, 796 yards (130 g) of DK-weight (#3 light)
black angora for polka dots and embroidery, small amount of worsted-weight (#4 medium)

Notions

Polyester stuffing

Hook

C/2 (2.75 mm)

Spotted Bull

Do not stuff ears. Sew to head with ears drooping downward.

Polka Dot Pattern (M)

Stuff head softly.

satin stitch

satin stitch

straight stitch

Add more stuffing to bottom of body to create rotund shape.

Stuff arms softly and add more stuffing for hands.

Stuff legs softly and add more stuffing for feet.

Height: About 19" (48 cm)

Make the Cheeks

When you stuff, gather from the inside.

Pull the cheeks and stuff.

Loosely embroider the mouth, creating curves at the tip of the mouth.

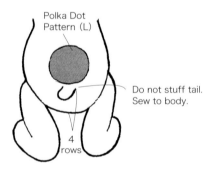

Polka Dot Pattern (L)

Do not stuff tail. Sew to body.

4 rows

Make the Spotted Bull

1. Crochet each part.

2. Stuff each part, except the ears and tail. Make sure to use the wrong side of the single crochet as the outside fabric.

3. Shape the cheeks, as shown in the diagram on page 78. Embroider the eyes, nose, and mouth, as shown in the diagram on page 78.

4. Sew all parts together, as shown on page 49. Sew the tail to the back, according to the diagram on page 78.

5. Crochet the polka dots and sew them to the top of the head and the lower back.

Crochet the Legs

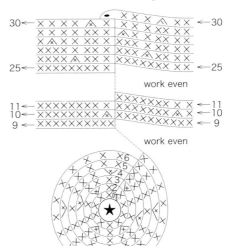

Legs
Make 2

row	sc	
30	12	(−2)
29	14	
28	14	(−2)
27	16	
26	16	(−2)
25		
⌇	18 work even	
11		
10	18	(−2)
9		
⌇	20 work even	
6		
5	20	(+2)
4	18	(+2)
3	16	(+2)
2	14	(+4)
1	10	skr

Crochet the Ears

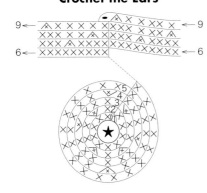

Ears
Make 2

row	sc	
9	12	(−2)
8	14	(−2)
7	16	(−2)
6	18	
5	18	
4	18	(+2)
3	16	(+2)
2	14	(+4)
1	10	skr

Crochet the Arms

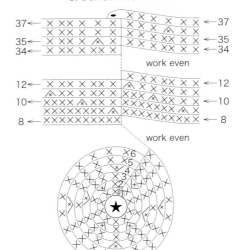

Arms
Make 2

row	sc	
37	12	
36	12	(−1)
35	13	(−1)
34		
⌇	14 work even	
12		
11	14	(−2)
10	16	(−2)
9	18	(−2)
8		
⌇	20 work even	
6		
5	20	(+2)
4	18	(+2)
3	16	(+2)
2	14	(+4)
1	10	skr

Crochet the Body

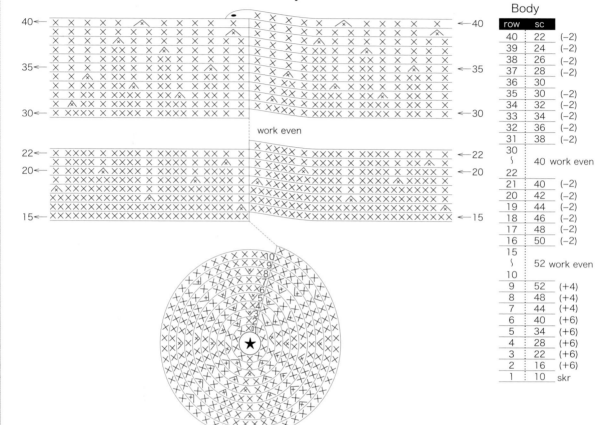

work even

Body

row	sc	
40	22	(−2)
39	24	(−2)
38	26	(−2)
37	28	(−2)
36	30	
35	30	(−2)
34	32	(−2)
33	34	(−2)
32	36	(−2)
31	38	(−2)
30 ⟩ 22	40	work even
21	40	(−2)
20	42	(−2)
19	44	(−2)
18	46	(−2)
17	48	(−2)
16	50	(−2)
15 ⟩ 10	52	work even
9	52	(+4)
8	48	(+4)
7	44	(+4)
6	40	(+6)
5	34	(+6)
4	28	(+6)
3	22	(+6)
2	16	(+6)
1	10	skr

Crochet the Tail

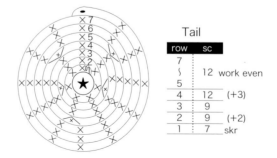

Tail

row	sc	
7 ⟩ 5	12	work even
4	12	(+3)
3	9	
2	9	(+2)
1	7	skr

Crochet the Head

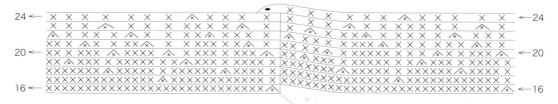

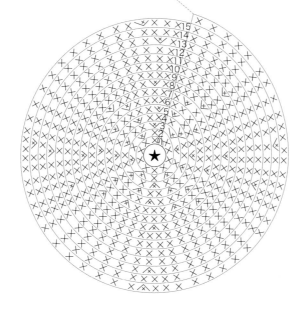

Head

row	sc	
24	24	(−2)
23	26	(−4)
22	30	(−6)
21	36	(−6)
20	42	(−6)
19	48	(−4)
18	52	(−4)
17	56	(−2)
16	58	(−2)
15	60	(+2)
14	58	(+2)
13	56	(+2)
12	54	(+2)
11	52	
10	52	(+2)
9	50	(+2)
8	48	(+4)
7	44	(+4)
6	40	(+6)
5	34	(+6)
4	28	(+6)
3	22	(+6)
2	16	(+6)
1	10	skr

Crochet the Polka Dots

Polka Dot Pattern (L)

row	sc	
5	42	(+8)
4	34	(+8)
3	26	(+8)
2	18	(+8)
1	10	skr

Polka Dot Pattern (M)

row	sc	
3	26	(+8)
2	18	(+8)
1	10	skr

Fluffy Poodle

Project shown on page 34

Materials

Yarn

ivory, beige, or brown bouclé yarn for body,
154 yards (150 g) of bulky-weight (#5 bulky)
black wool for embroidery, small amount of fingering-weight (#1 superfine)

Notions

Two ⅓" (8 mm) black eye buttons
Polyester stuffing

Hook

C/2 (2.75 mm)

Make the Fluffy Poodle

1. Crochet each part.

2. Stuff each part, except the ears. Make sure to use the wrong side of the single crochet as the outside fabric.

3. Attach the eyes. Embroider the nose and mouth, as shown in the diagram at right.

4. Sew all parts together, as shown on page 49. Sew the tail to the back, as shown in the diagram below. For the ivory poodle, embroider the hands and feet.

Fluffy Poodle

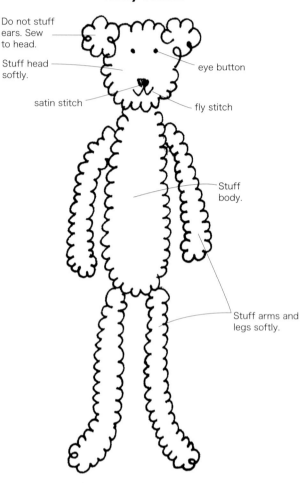

Do not stuff ears. Sew to head.

Stuff head softly.

eye button

satin stitch

fly stitch

Stuff body.

Stuff arms and legs softly.

Height: About 19" (48 cm)

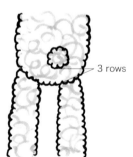

3 rows

straight stitch

For the ivory poodle, straight stitch on hands and feet.

Tail

← 1

sc 7

Crochet the Head

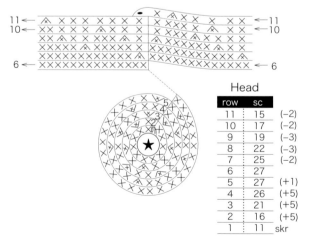

Head

row	sc	
11	15	(−2)
10	17	(−2)
9	19	(−3)
8	22	(−3)
7	25	(−2)
6	27	
5	27	(+1)
4	26	(+5)
3	21	(+5)
2	16	(+5)
1	11	skr

Crochet the Legs

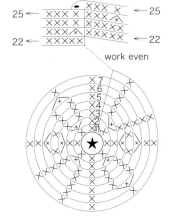

Legs
Make 2

row	sc	
25	8	
24	8	(−1)
23	9	(−1)
22		
⌇	10	work even
7		
6	10	(−2)
5	12	(−2)
4	14	
3	14	(+2)
2	12	(+4)
1	8	skr

work even

Crochet the Ears

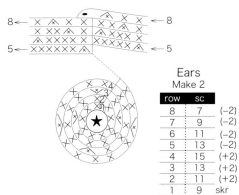

Ears
Make 2

row	sc	
8	7	(−2)
7	9	(−2)
6	11	(−2)
5	13	(−2)
4	15	(+2)
3	13	(+2)
2	11	(+2)
1	9	skr

Crochet the Body

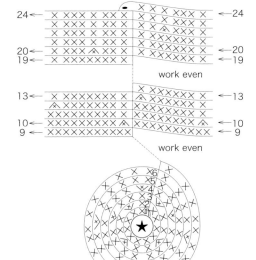

work even

work even

Body

row	sc	
24	15	
23	15	
22	15	(−1)
21	16	
20	16	(−1)
19		
⌇	17	work even
13		
12	17	(−2)
11	19	
10	19	(−2)
9		
⌇	21	work even
6		
5	21	(+2)
4	19	(+2)
3	17	(+2)
2	15	(+4)
1	11	skr

Crochet the Arms

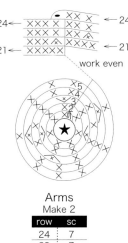

work even

Arms
Make 2

row	sc	
24	7	
23	7	
22	7	(−2)
21		
⌇	9	work even
5		
4	9	(−2)
3	11	(+2)
2	9	(+2)
1	7	skr

Zigzag Pig

Project shown on page 38

Materials

Yarn

white chenille for body, 459 yards (75 g) of DK-weight (#3 light)
black mohair for stripes, 79 yards (20 g) of sport-weight (#2 fine)
black wool for shoes and embroidery, 44 yards (10 g) of fingering-weight (#1 superfine)

Notions

Two ⅓" (8 mm) black eye buttons
Polyester stuffing

Hook

B/1 (2.25 mm)
C/2 (2.75 mm)

Make the Zigzag Pig

1. Crochet each part. Use a C/2 (2.75 mm) crochet hook, except for the shoes. Use a B/1 (2.25 mm) crochet hook for the shoes.

2. Stuff each part, except for the ears. Make sure to use the wrong side of the single crochet as the outside fabric, except for the shoes. Use the right side for the shoes.

3. Attach the eyes and nose to the head. Embroider the nose and mouth, as shown in the diagram below.

4. Sew all parts together, as shown on page 49. Sew the tail to the back, according to the diagram below.

5. Slip the shoes onto the feet.

Zigzag Pig

Do not stuff ears. Sew to head.

Stuff nose.

straight stitch

eye button

Stuff head softly.

Stuff body and hands softly.

Stuff legs softly.

Put on shoes.

Height: About 21¾" (55 cm)

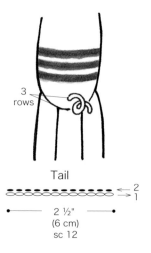

3 rows

Tail

2 ½" (6 cm)
sc 12

2
1

Crochet the Head

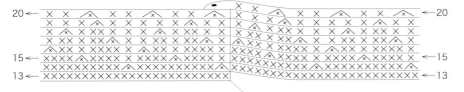

Head

row	sc	
20	18	(−6)
19	24	(−4)
18	28	(−4)
17	32	(−4)
16	36	(−4)
15	40	(−4)
14	44	(−4)
13	48	
12	48	
11	48	(+2)
10	46	(+2)
9	44	(+2)
8	42	(+2)
7	40	(+2)
6	38	(+4)
5	34	(+6)
4	28	(+6)
3	22	(+6)
2	16	(+6)
1	10	skr

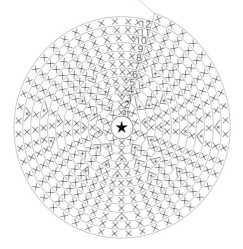

Crochet the Ears

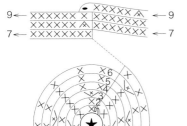

Ears
Make 2

row	sc	
9	13	(−1)
8	14	(−1)
7	15	
6	15	
5	15	(+2)
4	13	(+2)
3	11	(+2)
2	9	(+2)
1	7	skr

Crochet the Nose

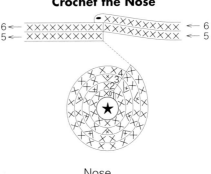

Nose

row	sc	
6		
⟩	20 work even	
4		
3	20	(+5)
2	15	(+5)
1	10	skr

Crochet the Arms

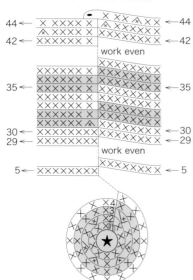

Arms
Make 2

color	row	sc	
white	44	12	(−1)
	43	13	(−2)
	42 ~ 37	15 work even	
black	36	15	
	35	15	
white	34	15	
	33	15	
black	32	15	
	31	15	(−1)
white	30 ~ 5	16 work even	
	4	16	
black	3	16	
	2	16	(+6)
	1	10	skr

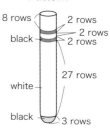

Striped Arm Pattern

8 rows — 2 rows
black — 2 rows — 2 rows
white — 27 rows
black — 3 rows

Crochet the Body

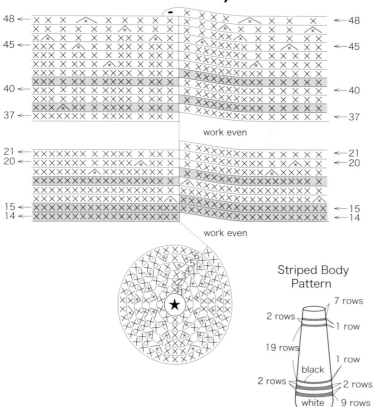

Body

color	row	sc	
white	48	17	(−2)
	47	19	(−3)
	46	22	(−3)
	45	25	(−3)
	44	28	
	43	28	(−2)
	42	30	
black	41	30	
white	40	30	
	39	30	
black	38	30	(−1)
white	37 ~ 21	31 work even	
	20	31	(−2)
	19	33	(−2)
black	18	35	
white	17	35	(−1)
	16	36	(−2)
black	15	38	
	14	38	
white	13	38	
	12	38	
black	11	38	
	10	38	
white	9 ~ 6	38 work even	
	5	38	(+6)
	4	32	(+7)
	3	25	(+7)
	2	18	(+8)
	1	10	skr

Striped Body Pattern

7 rows
2 rows — 1 row
19 rows
1 row
black
2 rows — 2 rows
white — 9 rows

Crochet the Shoes

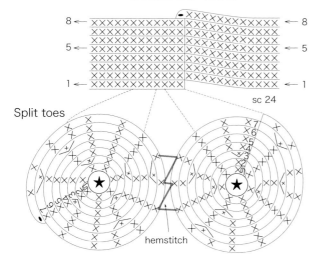

8 ← XXXX... → 8
5 ← XXXX... → 5
1 ← XXXX... → 1

sc 24

Split toes

hemstitch

Split Toes
Make 2

row	sc	
7	15	
6	15	(+2)
5	13	(+2)
4	11	
3	11	(+2)
2	9	(+2)
1	7	skr

Shoes

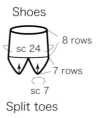

sc 24 — 8 rows
7 rows
sc 7

Split toes

Crochet the Legs

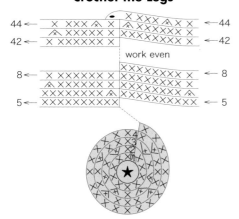

44 ← X XXX ⋀ X → 44
42 ← X XXXXX X → 42

work even

8 ← X XXXXX X → 8
5 ← XXXXXXXX → 5

Legs
Make 2

color	row	sc	
	44	13	(−2)
	43	15	(−2)
white	42		
	⟩	17	work even
	25		
black	24	17	
	23	17	
white	22	17	
	21	17	
black	20	17	
	19	17	
	18		
	⟩	17	work even
white	8		
	7	17	(−1)
	6	18	(−(2)
	5	20	
	4	20	
black	3	20	(+4)
	2	16	(+6)
	1	10	skr

Striped Pattern for Legs

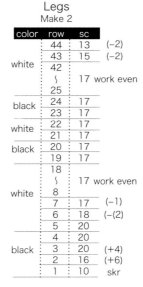

white — 20 rows
black — 2 rows
2 rows
2 rows
14 rows — white
black — 4 rows

Traveling Clothes: Scarf, Hat, and Bag

Project shown on page 40

Materials

Yarn

white chenille, 796 yards (130 g) of DK-weight (#3 light)
black angora, small amount of worsted-weight (#4 medium)

Hook

C/2 (2.75 mm)

Make the Traveling Clothes

Scarf: Chain 8 stitches. Single crochet these stitches, alternating colors every two rows to create stripes. Tie yarn at both ends to create fringe.

Bag: Crochet each part. To make the polka dots, use the Polka Dot Pattern on page 69. To make the handle, refer to the scarf pattern on page 64, but use 20 stitches. Make sure to use the right side of the single crochet as the outside fabric. Sew the handle and the polka dots to the bag.

Hat: Crochet the hat, alternating colors to create stripes. Make a 1¼" (3 cm) in diameter pom-pom using both colors of yarn (refer to page 50) and attach the pom-pom to the tip of the hat.

Crochet the Scarf

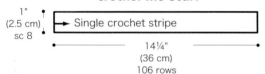

1"
(2.5 cm)
sc 8

Single crochet stripe

14¼"
(36 cm)
106 rows

Single crochet stripe

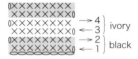

ivory
black

Crochet the Bag

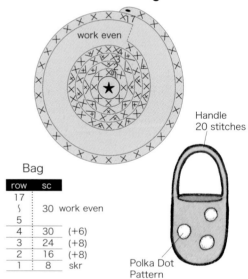

work even

Handle
20 stitches

Polka Dot Pattern

Bag

row	sc	
17		
∫	30	work even
5		
4	30	(+6)
3	24	(+8)
2	16	(+8)
1	8	skr

Crochet the Hat

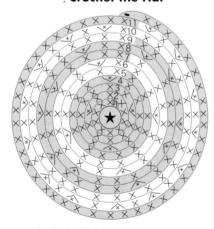

Hat

color	row	sc	
black	11	42	
ivory	10	42	(+14)
	9	28	
black	8	28	(+6)
	7	22	(+4)
ivory	6	18	(+2)
	5	16	(+2)
	4	14	(+1)
black	3	13	(+1)
	2	12	(+2)
	1	10	skr

Attach pom-pom to top of hat.